ASPECTS OF MEIJI MODERNIZATION

D1526664

Students and faculty at Nanko, a predecessor of Tokyo Imperial University, 1871.

ASPECTS OF MEIJI MODERNIZATION

The Japan Helpers and the Helped

Clark L. Beck and Ardath W. Burks, editors

Distributed by Transaction Books
New Brunswick (U.S.A.) and London (U.K.)

New Brunswick, New Jersey
Archibald Stevens Alexander Library
Rutgers, The State University of New Jersey
1983

The publication of this book was made possible, in part, by a grant from the New Jersey Committee for the Humanities, through the National Endowment for the Humanities.

Library of Congress Cataloging in Publication Data
Main entry under title:

Aspects of Meiji modernization.

Essays which originated as papers presented at a symposium held at Rutgers in Dec. 1980.
Includes bibliographical references.
1. Technical assistance — Japan — History — Congresses.
2. Japan — History — Meiji period, 1868-1912 — Congresses.
I. Beck, Clark L., 1945-   II. Burks, Ardath W.
HC462.7.A84   1983   338.952   83-8707
ISBN 0-87855-936-1 (pbk.)

TABLE OF CONTENTS

FOREWORD

This slim volume of essays, which centers on aspects of the modernization of Japan during the Meiji era a century ago, originated in a symposium held at Rutgers, the State University of New Jersey, in December 1980. The panel discussion in turn helped launch an exhibition of materials drawn from Special Collections -- mainly the voluminous Griffis Papers -- of the Alexander Library. The exhibit, which was displayed from December 6, 1980 to March 15, 1981, and published catalogue were prepared by the editors of this volume.

The formal opening of the exhibit and attendant symposium marked a kind of academic celebration of the ties between Rutgers and Japan, a contact which has lasted for one hundred and eighteen years. A number of friends of the library, colleagues from sister institutions, and dignitaries were present. Among the latter were Ambassador Takahashi Shotaro, Consul General of Japan-New York, and a small delegation from Japan, including Mayor Ohtake Yukio of Fukui City and President Igarashi Tadao of Fukui University. The following year, the two universities -- Rutgers and Fukui -- signed an agreement for cultural and educational exchange.

At the time of the original symposium, in 1980, a number of those present felt that the papers presented constituted a contribution to the understanding of American-Japanese relations and their background. The presentations were revised into the form of essays, with appropriate documentation.

We are grateful, of course, to our colleagues who originally participated in the symposium. Publication of their essays was made possible by the further generosity of, and support from, the New Jersey Committee for the Humanities (an affiliate of the National Endowment for the Humanities) and the Rutgers

University Libraries. The International Center of Rutgers University, under the direction of Dr. Jessie Lutz, aided in preparation of the manuscript.

Hendrik Edelman
University Librarian

New Brunswick, New Jersey
April 1, 1982

INTRODUCTION

by Ardath W. Burks

Both at home and abroad, there has been renewed interest in the late nineteenth century transition of Japan from an almost completely isolated feudal society to a dynamic nation. As Marius Jansen indicates, in his essay in this volume, there have been few, if any, parallels in the experiences of the non-Atlantic world.

There have been those who have sought in the Japanese case a guide to the yet developing world. Indeed, more recently Japan's successes have led to the suggestion that the nation has dealt so well with modernity as to serve as a model for advanced industrial democracies.[1] It may well be, however, that the Japanese experience has in fact been unique and, therefore, not readily transferable. It has nonetheless remained of interest for its own sake, yet another variable alongside the constant dynamic of history.

In any case, the Japanese leaders who guided the transformation a century ago have received continued attention. Beyond doubt, the tightly knit establishment which guides the contemporary super-power from Tokyo is directly descended from a leadership corps which steered Japan into and through the changes of the nineteenth century. The Meiji era (1868-1912) is in turn recognized as child of the Tokugawa period (1600-1867), whose society was far better prepared for participation in the modernization process than had been realized at the time.

Of almost equal interest, at least in Japan, is the story of those foreign visitors who were present to witness the changes and who, in greater or lesser degree, helped the Japanese in the transition. Revived interest in the (Meiji) transition, in the Meiji modernizers (the "helped," described by Jansen), and in the foreigners (the "Japan helpers," as John Maki calls them in his essay) has focused attention on some perennial problems in interpreting Japanese history.

1

Shall we emphasize the decay and regeneration of indigenous (Japanese) institutions, or the impact and effects of foreign (in this case, Western) influence?[2] Put another way, does the Japanese society (as many have claimed) display a certain unique, non-erosive core, which resists or at least smooths out alien influence? Or, is Japanese development (as others have argued) not at all exotic, lending itself readily to analysis under the laws of history?

In similar fashion, some (usually Japanese) observers have placed an emphasis approaching hero worship on the role of the native "founding fathers," neglecting both foreigners' contributions and the considerable work of sub-leaders in Japanese society. Others (usually outsiders, but including some Japanese) have assigned an exaggerated role to the foreigners employed by the new Meiji government in the transition.

Recent scholarship has tended to mix the two influences: the slow, evolutionary culture change (from the "post-feudal" Tokugawa to the Meiji era) and the rapid, revolutionary culture contact (with the West). Difficult questions can be begged by agreeing at least that the Meiji leadership and the foreign employees often thought that they were involved in the process of change as renovationists (or "modernizers," although this word smacks of recent controversy).[3] Most would agree, in any case, that the final result of the Meiji transition was not the "Westernization" of Japan.

The arrival of foreigners--most notably, Commodore Matthew Calbraith Perry in his "black ships"-- was the occasion for, not the basic cause of, Japan's transformation in the nineteenth century. The climax came, some one hundred and fourteen years ago, with the so-called Meiji Restoration (1868), which in turn paved the way for the modernization of Japan.

It must be remembered, however, that in the earliest stage of the transition, the thrust was to protect Japan against threatening Western power. One of the most popular slogans was "to strengthen the army, to enrich the country."* Satsuma and Choshu among the so-called outer domains were brilliantly manipulated by sub-leaders (the lower-rank samurai), who believed that the way to meet the threat was to achieve military and political equality with foreign powers. In other words, they turned to advanced military and economic techniques in order to avoid Western influence at the core of Japanese society.

On January 3, 1868, a coalition of Satsuma, Choshu, and other outer domains announced in the name of the Emperor the resumption of what was called Imperial rule. The various steps taken thereafter by the Meiji modernizers have been featured in the general histories of Japan.[4]

---

*fukoku-kyohei

In brief summary, in 1869 the new regime maneuvered the lords (of feudal domains) into returning land registers to the Emperor. In most cases, the former lords simply became the Emperor's governors of the domains. In the decade that followed, the entire political, economic, and social structure was redesigned. In 1871, the last vestiges of formal feudalism were surgically removed, an operation witnessed by the young William Elliot Griffis. As one of the early foreign employees, who had taught some of the first Japanese students overseas (at Rutgers College) and who was then in Japan (in Fukui), he observed and described the transformation.[5]

Next, in 1872 came the fundamental law on education (to be followed later by the Imperial Rescript on Education). Thereby every Japanese son and daughter was to become a trained subject of the Emperor. Every Japanese became a modern man also through the Imperial Rescript on military conscription in 1873. Similarly, in the same year he gained thoroughly modern status by becoming eligible for taxation directly by the central government. By 1873 the reformers, the Meiji modernizers, had moved into positions of leadership. By 1875 they had arrested Western expansion and guaranteed Japan's subsequent escape from the unequal treaty status to be suffered by China for decades thereafter.

Meanwhile, the government itself was being streamlined and centralized with the addition of ministries of finance, army, navy, foreign, and home affairs, and a court and legal system. In the economic realm, banks were established, lighthouses were built, and port facilities improved. Government-sheltered strategic industries were nurtured and privately-financed small-scale businesses encouraged. Even the frontier of Hokkaido was developed, perhaps the only case of true Westernization as the northern island took on an American appearance complete with range lines, silos, and cattle herds.

Several aspects of this remarkable transformation deserve mention so that we may understand the context of the essays which follow. Early on, the Meiji government (following in the footsteps of the late Tokugawa shogunate) turned to a vigorous search for knowledge and technology available in the West. One of the first clear signposts indicating the new direction to be taken was the famous Charter Oath of April 1868.[6]

Of special interest in the interaction of Japanese leadership and Western know-how was the Iwakura Embassy, detailed by Marius Jansen in his essay below. Its chief characteristic (sounding the tone of the era which the mission symbolized) was optimism. Like many modernizers, the Meiji leaders had come to believe in the desirability, even the inevitability, of change and, of course, any change (they thought) was for the better.

Incidentally, in one sense Japan was not (as has often been claimed) a late developer. In the drive for "civilization and enlightment,"* Japan plunged directly into highly specialized streams flowing in nineteenth century Western cultures. As Hazel Jones put it, "the cultural-educational childhood was skipped over."[7] And yet in Japan a dual ideology persisted: "Eastern spirit-Western technology."[+]

To carry out all the innovations the men of Meiji mobilized domestic resources and sought out Western knowledge. Both at home and abroad, the Japanese became engaged in one of the most significant experiments in massive borrowing the world has ever seen. In what today would be called a process of seeking technical assistance, the Japanese had several options.

Of the alternatives, the two swiftest and most available were also the least desirable: use of alien capital in the form of loans and the employment of foreigners as teachers, assistants, and advisers. A third method was to import educational materials and to translate them. In doing so, the Meiji actually was following in the shadow of the Tokugawa regime in its last days. During the early Meiji, however, the flow of materials picked up noticeably so that the era became known as the "age of translation." This method did result in a kind of Westernization. The process was, however, slow and constituted a second-hand contact.

The employment of foreigners and a fourth means, the despatch of student abroad,[@] soon took precedence over translation. This last method, the movement of Japanese students abroad, was favored because it allowed direct observation of foreign cultures. Moreover, it began the process of training what Robert Schwantes has called in modern terminology the Japanese "counterparts" of employed foreigners. The natives soon displaced the aliens.[8]

It has been estimated that the Meiji government issued over 11,000 (or 3 percent of all) passports for study abroad in the period 1868-1902. In the same span of time, some 900 Japanese studied in American institutions of higher education, distributed among over 100 universities, colleges, and seminaries. In the 1870's, they congregated in the East: at Rutgers College, the United States Naval Academy, Yale, and Harvard. In the 1880's they drifted to the mid-west and in the 1890's, to the West coast, where the concentration is still great today.[9]

---

*bummei kaika
+wakon-yosai
@In popular parlance, the term was kaigai ryugaku (travel abroad), used for various purposes including study abroad. In official use, ryugakusei was narrower in meaning and referred to formal study abroad.

4

In Japan something over a century ago alien advisers, assistants, and foreign teachers were the forerunners of the modern Peace Corps. In any given year during the Meiji period, the number of foreigners in Japan for all purposes and under a variety of auspices was a fairly constant 8,000. Fully half of these were Chinese, who worked as ordinary laborers. It has been estimated that official, government-sponsored foreign employees* numbered about 3,000. They gave to the Meiji government some 9,500 man-years of counsel and aid (broken down as follows: British, over 4,300; French, about 1,500; Germans and Americans, each, about 1,200).[10] Throughout its decade of operation the Commission for Hokkaido Development (Kaitakushi or Colonization Commission) was served mainly by Americans, who were engaged in surveying, mining, rail construction, soil improvement, dairy farming, fruit and grain experimentation.

Griffis, who came to Japan in 1871 to work for a domain and later, for the Meiji government until 1874, described his early American colleagues. It was Dr. S. Wells Williams, he wrote, who beseeched the missionary societies to send to "a proud-spirited people, who 'wanted everything from the West, except opium and Christianity'," only wise teachers. Four "elect Americans" -- Guido Verbeck, Samuel R. Brown, Channing Moore Williams, and James C. Hepburn, "of finest culture and noblest spirit"[11] -- were chosen and reached Yokohama in the autumn of 1859.

Not all the early foreigners were cultured or of noble spirit. The Japanese turned to setting standards for employment first in the field of education and in this project, Verbeck played a crucial role.+ As head teacher of the new liberal arts school+, he began an immediate housecleaning to rid the system of port drunks and refugees from forecastles. By February 1870, the government[12] had drafted its Instructions for Hiring Foreigners and shortly thereafter, the term "foreign employees" was in general currency. By then too, certain distinctions had been made among all "hired help," those engaged under private auspices, and government employees.@ By the late 1880's, all the first generation government employees were being phased out as their contracts expired.

---

* oyatoi gaikokujin (the term as such was probably first used in 1872).
+ Daigaku nanko, one of the forerunners of Tokyo Imperial University (now known as The University of Tokyo).
@ yatoi ("hired help"); shiyatoi (private auspices); kanyatoi (government auspices); and oyatoi gaikokujin (the general term).

Now much more needs to be done in the realm of motivation of these hired foreigners, even though such study would involve psychobiography on a case-by-case basis. In historical perspective, on some occasions motives had sprung from feelings of god, gold, and glory (the Iberians); or arose from queen and country (the British); or contained a sense of mission (the Americans). Out of the subtle mixture of Christianity, nationalism, and profiteering emerged, in other parts of Asia, the white man's burden, imperialism, and colonialism.[13] In China and in Japan, equipped with estabished governments, the result was rather, what Mao Tse-tung called "semi-colonialism."

The hired foreigners variously saw themselves as "sojourners in Lotus-Land," as "creators of the New Japan," or simply as "hired help." As might be expected, those who played a low-key role and willingly faded into the advisory background behind the screen (like Verbeck, in Japan 1859-1898, and Henry Willard Dennison, in Japan 1874-1914), were the most successful. Benjamin Smith Lyman, as Fujita Fumiko points out in her essay, was a refreshing case: he admitted openly what other foreigners tended to camouflage, namely, his purposes in going to Japan. They were in part to expand the frontiers of scientific knowledge (the advisers who concentrated on this task were mostly successful); in part, to gain fame and remuneration. In an unguarded letter Griffis also frankly stated his objectives: while in Japan, he could study on his theology; he could collect materials to write a book; he could support his family at home, "at least pay the rent," carpet the floors, and eventually obtain a handsome home![14]

Regardless of the varying motives, some of the hired foreigners (Griffis, Verbeck, David Murray, and Ernest Fenollosa, for example) at the very beginning of their stint realized that it was the Japanese who were setting the goals, paying for and managing the technical assistance, and implementing the policies of directed change. Because the Japanese early asserted firm control in the enterprise, the foreigners' role was in the opinion of Hazel Jones, probably not parasitic but symbiotic.[15] As Donald Roden points out in his essay, the Americans at least, as cultural missionaries tended to reflect an attitude of diplomatic idealism characteristic of United States policy of that era. Under the firm control of the Meiji regime, however, they too tended to bolster emerging Japanese state ideologies. Finally, the employed foreigners performed decision-conditioning, rather than decision-making, roles. Despite the aura of glamor thrown around them, then and now, their contribution in Japan was marginal.

Again as Roden explains, the historical significance of these foreigners lay in, not so much what they accomplished, as in what they saw and described first-hand. They were in an enviable position to detail for informed, curious countrymen this strange land and to identify steps in its transition. Granted, they often carried to Japan in their luggage certain nineteenth century prejudices of culture, race, and politics. Americans in particular, then as now, felt a sense of mission to "save" the Japanese, whether the attitude was specifically religious (among the missionary-educators) or secular (among those who simply offered technical assistance). It is to the credit of the perceptive that on occasion they went beyond ethnocentric, normative judgment and directly described what they saw.

One can choose from among the foreign personalities, some quite flamboyant, Lafcadio Hearn because, as Maki states, he was the effective popularizer. It would be difficult to exaggerate the influences of Hearn in projecting an exotic image of the remote island-nation. Or one can center on Griffis because in studious fashion he introduced many knowledgeable Americans of the nineteenth century · to Japan. (His prose too tended to border on the purple.) In his essay, John Maki concentrates on William Smith Clark because among the Japanese he remains the most widely known, despite his stay of less than a year. The impact of Clark on the region of Hokkaido was enormous (it is still visible today) and, therefore, he may be the exception.

It is significant that Clark, on his return to Amherst, Massachusetts, frequently spoke in public, often making comparisons unfavorable to his own society. As Robert A. Rosenstone has pointed out, many of the Americans-resident-in-Japan found admirable traits in the social practices of this Asian nation. He has written:

> Their articles, books, letters, journals, and diaries abound with favorable responses to the skills, values, and traditions of the native culture. Some things seemed so worthwhile that admiration shaded into the desire to emulate and occasionally into the claim that Japan was a land that could teach as well as learn from the West.[16]

From other points of view (outside their perennial contractual difficulties), Japan left many Americans in a state of comparative cultural discomfort. As Americans on a mission, they were not prepared for a society that could call some of their basic values into question, not yet ready for a nation that was not quite economically developed but could seem to be in some ways more civilized than was the United States.[17]

To return to the employed foreigners and their role in Japan, there was a marked ambivalence in their experience, which has been felt by all Japan hands since. The early ecstatic enthusiasm upon arrival often gave way to frustrating friction the longer the stay. Fujita Fumiko has concentrated on this fascinating aspect of cultural exchange, most often neglected in anniversary celebrations of contact. Benjamin Smith Lyman's career, as described below, admirably illustrates the tension. Griffis fortunately soon forgot the quarrels over his last contract.

Indeed it is surprising, as Fujita concludes, that with all the difficulties on both sides -- "everywhere was tension, fatigue, and the cry for relief," one employee put it -- by and large the foreigners left "stable, warm feelings." This was particularly true in Hokkaido, in attitudes toward the irrascible Lyman and the efficient Clark.

NOTES

1. See Ezra Vogel, Japan As Number One: Lessons for America (Cambridge, Mass.: Harvard University Press, 1979).

2. The question has been spelled out by John Whitney Hall, "Introduction: Japan's Historical Position," Japan: From Pre-History to Modern Times (New York: Dell, 1970),chap. 1.

3. Professor Sakata Yoshio, formerly Kyoto University, made the useful distinction between restoration (osei fukko) of the Meiji Emperor and renovation (ishin) of the Japanese society.

4. Parts of this introduction have been adapted from a catalogue prepared for the exhibition of materials from Special Collections, Alexander Library, Rutgers University (December 6, 1980-March 15, 1981); see Clark L. Beck & Ardath W. Burks, eds. As We Saw Them: Westerners Interpret Japan 1853-1912 (New Brunswick: Rutgers, the State University of New Jersey, 1980), "Introduction."

5. See the essay by Marius Jansen, below, and his n.4.

6. For the complete translated text of the Charter Oath (Gokajo no goseimon) see the essay by Marius Jansen and his n.1.

7. H. J. Jones, Live Machines: Hired Forieners and Meiji Japan (Vancover: University of British Columbia Press, 1980), p. 133.

8. The definitive study is Ishizuki Minoru, Kindai Nihon no kaigai-ryugaku (A history of overseas study in modern Japan) (Kyoto: 1972).

9. These estimates were drawn from James T. Conte, "Meiji Ryugakusei: Overseas Study in the Development of Japan, 1867-1902," paper prepared for the 28th Annual Meeting of the Association for Asian Studies, Toronto, Canada, March, 1976.

10. Jones, Live Machines, cited, p. 7.

11. W. E. Griffis, "Four Makers of Modern Japan" (unpublished manuscript), Department of Special Collections and Archives, Rutgers University Libraries.

12. Gaikokujin yatoi-irekata kokoroe no jojo, Meiji 3/2 Foreign Ministry Records Bureau, Tokyo (translated and included as Appendix 1 in Jones, Live Machines, cited, pp. 155-158).

13. Jones, Live Machines, cited, p. 71.

14. Letter, W. E. Griffis to Margaret Griffis, September 26, 1870, Department of Special Collections and Archives, Rutgers University Libraries.

15. Jones, Live Machines, cited, p. 129.

16. As to whether the Americans in Japan were typical or not, Rosenstone has left this historical judgment: "The Americans who left records of life in Japan were white, middle class, often college graduates, and, for the most part, engaged in professions like science, teaching, engineering, journalism, and the ministry." They were "the kind of people who manned the command posts of middle-class culture in the classroom, pulpit, government, and press and who thought of themselves as custodians of American values." See Robert A. Rosenstone, "Learning from Those 'Imitative' Japanese: Another Side of the American Experience in the Mikado's Empire," American Historical Review, v. 85, no. 3 (June 1980), 572-595, especially p. 574, n. 4.

17. Rosenstone, loc. cit., p. 595.

THE MEIJI MODERNIZERS

by Marius B. Jansen

The Meiji Period witnessed the transformation of an isolated, underdeveloped island country into a world power. A status-bound, feudal society became a dynamic nation in which advancement depended on ability developed through education. Divided and mutually suspicious domains were transformed into one of the most effectively centralized and unified countries. All in all, this was a process of state building and modernization that has few parallels, perhaps no real parallel, in the non-Atlantic world. Moreover, it was a program begun under unfavorable international conditions of unequal treaties, with restrictions on national sovereignty. Economic conditions too were unfavorable; the government had a heavy debt to assume, enforced limitations on tariff, and it began with technological backwardness. There was no Development Bank, no economic aid, no World Bank to which it could turn. One might almost say that it should not have been possible, and in fact it does not seem to have been possible anywhere else (with the possible exception of Russia).

Therefore an examination of the leaders and their program is of constant interest. So is the examination of those who saw it begin to happen, who helped it happen, and who first wrote about it. This is especially true of the Americans involved, for their work marked the beginning of a contact that has grown steadily in importance through trade, conflict, reconstruction, and now alliance and cooperation.

The great themes of Meiji modernization were set out in the so-called Charter Oath of April 1868:

- deliberative assemblies were to be set up, and matters would be conducted according to public opinion

11

- all classes were called upon to unite

- commoners and officials, both civil and military, should pursue their own calling

- evil customs were to be ended, and the "just laws of nature" would be used as standards for new institutions

- knowledge was to be sought throughout the world in order to strengthen the foundations of imperial rule.[1]

These ideas were stated with a generality that could alarm no specific group or region. They were meant initially to reassure the upper classes. Commoners, in fact, were instructed to carry on as before. And yet the Charter Oath served as authorization for the great reforms of the nineteenth century and even for the democratic reforms of the years after World War II. It has been referred to particularly frequently by the present emperor to explain that Japan is now again on the right track.

For the historian, on the other hand, it is also easy to see that the Charter Oath had specific connotations. Language about assemblies and public opinion contrasted to the monopolization of power by the Tokugawa rulers who had just been overthrown. Language about classes uniting, and about groups pursuing their own calling, suggested that the status divisions of late feudal society would give way to a more equitable arrangement. And the "evil customs" that were going to be replaced by "wisdom sought throughout the world" promised an end to the dual governments of court and camp, and the multiple governments of feudal domains, in a rearrangement that would put Japanese institutions in line with principles followed elsewhere in the world. Seeking such principles "throughout the world" guaranteed an end to the rigidity of a secluded and closed country and the anti-foreign frenzy of zealot swordsmen through which the country had just passed. Consequently we were justified in seeing this famous oath as a specific as well as a general statement of intent to modernize.

Contemporaries were quick to recognize the thrust of the Charter Oath. It is interesting to see William Elliott Griffis point to it in 1876 in The Mikado's Empire,[2] a book that was the chief source of information about Japan for Americans for a long time. The book had 12 editions by 1913, and it was reprinted as a classic as recently as 1971. Griffis combined his discussion on the Charter Oath with other themes that became part of a standard set of views about the Meiji changes.

He emphasized the intellectual preparation for imperial rule in national learning, and he played down the impact of western imperialism. He was full of admiration for the samurai who stepped forth to lead; four fifths of them were from the four southwestern domains, he said, but he also insisted that "natural ability asserts its power." He went on to describe them as men who were frustrated under feudalism, but also as men who get their training in government then, for "real power lay in hands of able men of inferior rank who ruled their masters"[3]; thus they were at once disadvantaged and advantaged.

And he was full of praise for the daimyo* - or at least most of them - who stepped down, making it possible for others to step forth.

> The writer counts among the most impressive
> of all his life's experiences that scene in the
> immense castle hall of Fukui, when the Daimio of
> Echizen bid farewell to his three thousand two-
> sworded retainers, and, amidst the tears and
> smiles and loving farewells of the city's popu-
> lace, left behind him lands, revenue and obedient
> followers, and retired to live as a private
> gentleman in Tokio.[4]

He surely had the greatest respect for the young emperor. He was "the cement" that made it possible to bind the country together and he might yet "become as much the real ruler of his people as the Czar." And finally, Griffis had little or nothing to say about the Japanese people. In this process, he thought, they were the clay to be shaped by their leaders. It may be useful to quote his summary:

> ... the true explanation of the events of the last
> eight years in Japan is to be sought in these ten-
> dencies and the internal history of the nation;
> the shogun, bakufu,[+] and perhaps even feudalism
> would have fallen, had foreigners never landed in
> Japan; the movement toward modern civilization
> originated from within, and not simply the result
> of foreign impact or pressure; the work of enlight-
> enment and education, which alone could assure
> success to the movememt, was begun and carried on
> by native students, statesmen, and simple
> patriots.[5]

---

* daimyo, a feudal lord.
+ shogun, the military dictatorship held by the Tokugawa family; bakufu, the military headquarters of the shogun.

These were views very similar to those of post-Restoration official historiography in Japan. As the Meiji years went on emphasis on the emperor grew, and with it Griffis' emphasis on him in later editions, until he concluded that he would "place him among the really great men of our age." But basically his was a picture of patriotic young leaders whose wise and judicious guidance for a backward population brought broadened participation through education and limited political privileges. His picture accorded well with the self-image of official Japan. It is still an important place to begin thinking about the Meiji changes, and we recognize these same notes in any good post-war history. But other notes have been added. New questions, and new access and new freedoms, have permitted additional emphases that are essential to the consideration of Japan's modernization.

The most important of these is certainly the view that the emperor system which Griffis saw as constructive and in fact essential has received more ambivalent estimates from historians who know what it led to in the 1930's. By extension the Meiji modernizers have begun to look like statists as well as statesmen, and that in turn has led to questions about what it was that they had to work with in their society and the degree to which they deserved their own self image. Did they really do it all alone? The answer, inevitably, is that they did not, and the result is a picture of the Japanese people in the nineteenth century that shows a society much richer, more varied, and more interesting, than even Griffis could have known.

It was a society better prepared for participation than any had realized. Education was more diffused, and literacy more widespread, than had been thought. Over half the males, and probably at least one tenth of Japanese females, were getting education outside their homes in a structured school setting. The building of schools was on the rise throughout the entire nineteenth century, and Meiji universal education programs represented a logical continuation of this trend. The Japanese people were a constituency that could be reached by its leaders, and it quickly shared their goals.

There was also a tide of change and reform in late Tokugawa days that saw the shogunate, in the fifteen years between the coming of Perry and its fall in 1868, try to do many of the things the new government would do later. It was sending students and missions abroad, and it was experimenting with some sort of conscription system instead of samurai levies and showing signs of a rational program of change led by its own "young samurai" -- petty vassals and minor daimyo in the various domains.

As to participation, Professor Irokawa and other "populist" historians have produced evidence of local leaders' close attention to national affairs that shows that they were anything but clay waiting to be shaped by a wise central government. In the 1870's and 1880's there were numerous, probably hundreds, of debating and discussion societies throughout the countryside; their members collected translations of western books on government, compared drafts of constitutions, studied the new treaties clause by clause, and occasionally produced drafts of constitutions that were far more liberal than the government's final product.[6]

In other words, the ferment of change went far beyond the leadership circles, and the directions proposed for the change were so broadly congruent that it was less a matter of what should be done than the speed with which it could be done; more who should lead, than where. The Charter Oath, by some uncanny alchemy, spoke for far more than the leaders by whom it was drawn up and to whom it was addressed.

All this need not diminish the importance and the role of the Meiji leaders. But it does reduce them to human size and to believable dimensions, at the same time that their countrymen take on a new dimension. Yet there is enough distinction and achievement for all involved in this program; enough daring and quickness of mind, and enough intelligence to permit us to retain the view that it was an extraordinary generation. Perhaps, indeed, we shall even conclude that the leaders were more remarkable still to maintain their ascendancy in such lively competition.

I find their experience of the West particulary instructive in this, and turn briefly to the Iwakura Embassy of the years 1871 to 1873. The Griffis collection in the Rutgers University Library includes numerous mementoes of that great embassy, including the pictures the leaders had taken on that occasion. The embassy was a twenty-one month world tour for the government leaders. How many leadership groups would have taken that chance? How many would have found their jobs waiting for them on their return? Yet here we had the top of the new government: Iwakura Tomomi, Okubo Toshimichi, Kido Takayoshi, Ito Hirobumi, and others. Each government department added members, and members had secretaries, commissioners, and officers. The recent feudal lords of Choshu, Saga, Fukuoka, Kanazawa went, of course, accompanied by their retainers; two court nobles went, and the Hokkaido Colonization Office sent representatives. Five young women were included to begin the education of women, and several dozen additional students went along. The total party thus came to number over 100. They used the still unfinished Yokohama railroad station for the sendoff.

The impact of this experience had to be enormous. Some
radicals found themselves sobered by the realization of the distance that separated Japan from the industrialized West, while
optimists took heart on learning that Western modernization was
of recent date. If one compared the Europe of today with that
of forty years ago, the chronicler of the embassy wrote, he
would find that there had been no trains, no steamers, no tele-
graphs, that small boats were pulled along canals, sails hoisted
at sea, and that horse-drawn carts still moved slowly along the
roads. But the embassy's Western hosts, then and later, also
warned them against precipitous measures. British Minister
Harry Parkes advised them to move with care, and General Grant
pointed out that liberties once granted could not easily be
withdrawn again. Herbert Spencer, whose prestige was enormous
in those decades, summed up this train of counsel two decades
later with a magisterial conclusion that "My advice is strongly
conservative in all directions."

The travelers restructured their heirarchy of nations during their trip. China, so long on top for Japanese esteem, had
to move aside to make way for the West. But that West turned
out to be a very complicated set of countries. Choice was possible, and in fact necessary. The mission's chronicler adopted
as his definition of civilization a simple correlation with the
distribution of the wealth produced by a country. Nothing could
better indicate the distance he had travelled from the feudal
society into which he had been born a samurai.

The Iwakura travellers spent their longest period, 205
days, in the United States. They were worried about the flaws
of an elective system and the way it might pander to the popular
and cheap, but impressed by the strength of associative institutions. America, their scribe recorded, seemed to have a happy
mix of resources and will, and this could probably be related to
its growth as the development ground for the independent-minded
from every nation in Europe. The United States quickly became a
magnet for Japanese students. Meiji Japan itself, in its development of the northern territory of Hokkaido, seemed a frontier
society, and Americans were soon hired to help with development,
agriculture, and education there.

But the political examples of central Europe, and particularly of a recently unified Germany, contained more appropriate
models for the travellers. The mission's narrative devoted more
space to Europe than to America. Russia, however, came off very
poorly. Its goods seemed crude, its trade was dominated by
foreigners, its government was autocratic and despotic, its
churches in their magnificence contrasted to the shocking
poverty of the peasants who made it all possible. Civilization,
the chronicler suggested, declined as one moved east.

What came out of this, then, was a view of the West more differentiated, and somehow less menacing, than the one it replaced. Japan had time. It had choices, and it should attend to internal reforms first. Germany and Austria had only recently worked out their institutions; America was still in process of formation. Japan, over all, was only some forty years behind the industrialization of the West.

Foreign travel could also give new meaning to the recent past, and even to the documents of that past. I am fascinated to find that the Charter Oath itself took on new meaning for Kido, who had helped to draft it, during his stay in Washington. Like his fellow ambassadors, he was to return to Japan convinced that some accomodation with representative institutions would be desirable in order to build a consensus for decisions in Japan; it was also important to align Japan with the most forward looking nations of the West. Kido's own wording for the Charter Oath had spoken of a council of feudal lords; but his colleagues had changed this to the more general wording calling for "deliberative councils broadly established." In Washington, however, he found the embassy scribe working on a translation of the United States Constitution. As they looked it over, they observed that Japan really ought to have some kind of state charter too. "Yes", responded Kume, the chronicler, "especially in view of the Emperor's promise." Kido seemed astonished; he asked for a copy, and the next morning rushed in to say that "Last night I read the Charter Oath very carefully, time after time. It is a superb document. We can never allow that spirit to change." And in his diary he went on to write that "In the first year of the Restoration we hastily worked out the five article Charter Oath and had it accepted by the leaders, feudal lords and court nobles, by way of setting out the direction for the future. But now it is time for us to have an unshakable fundamental law. From now on I want to concentrate my attention on matters such as the basic laws and government structure of other countries."[8]

If the Charter Oath meant more to Kido after four years, it has meant even more to his countrymen in later years. Kido did not live to see its expression in the Meiji Constitution of 1889, but his emperor's grandson finds in it authorization for the far more sweeping guarantees of liberty embodied in the present constitution of Japan.

The embassadors returned to Japan in 1873. They plunged immediately into sharp disputes about priorities for internal reform and foreign policies, and they had to struggle to enforce their will and lay out the path of cautious constitutional reform. Yet it says something about the shared values and purposes of the leadership group that it was possible for them to do this.

17

So it is interesting to look again at the faces of the young modernizers that are included in the Griffis collection, photographs taken in preparation for their journey around the world. These are young men, in their thirties and early forties. They are veterans of danger, but also full of curiosity about what they will see. And they are determined to create upon their return a country that will not have to accept second place to any.

Their conviction that this was possible brings us to another important feature of the period: its optimism. Japan would have its chance, and so would able individuals. Things were going to be better. This optimism also found expression in popular movements of renewal and utopian enthusiasm, and in religious cults emphasizing a better life here and now.

Ambition for the nation was paralleled by ambition for the individual. Samuel Smiles' Self Help was a best seller for the entire Meiji Period and long after. Limitations of status, rank, and region began to give way to qualifications established through education. There was a rush to Tokyo, the wonder city of the new and modern. There was faith in technology, in science, in reason, and in institutions. If early Meiji seems optimistic to us, it also seems naive. But after all it was a time that still had little knowledge of the destructive aspects of modern war or of environment degredation. Problems seemed solvable.

This optimism was fully shared by the outsiders who came to help, especially by Americans like Griffis who came in the years after the Civil War. Their optimism and their idealism was in a measure the product of a great war for freedom that had been won. It is sometimes tempting to compare their idealism with that of their successors in 1945 who shared some of that ebullience and enthusiasm in heightened form. For the early Occupationaires the wrongs of the old society were clear enough, and they were the enemies to be conquered.

Something of the sort was alive in Meiji too; the wrongs of the old society -- status, weakness, and a conservative past -- were all to be corrected swiftly by a new autonomous state.

The Meiji state they built did in fact correct many of them, though not without creating a few others and maintaining some in different form. As historians we can see what our Japanese colleagues mean when they point to those problems, to the new inequities, and criticize the movement for its flaws. But they, and we, now see with hindsight. That is why it is good to look again at the contemporary sources and faces, to get fresh impression of the records, and problems as contemporaries saw them. Those are strong faces on Kido, Okubo, and the others;

they are not afraid to make decisions, or to act, because they are quite sure of what they want to change.

Like their foreign employees, they see things with the sharp focus of youth and enthusiasm. That is why they speak to us so directly and so powerfully today. They were far from constituting the whole story of modern Japan, but they were certainly an important part of it. We understand them better now because we know more about their generation then we did. It was one that experienced a flood of change unlike anything earlier Japanese had known. And it did so with patience, dignity, and courage.

My colleague William Lockwood was fond of quoting Virginia Wedgewood. History is written backwards, she wrote, but lived forward, and it is very hard for those who know the ending to realize what is was like to know only the beginning. Of course we too are fortunately still far from knowing the ending. But we do know an ending different from the one our predecessors did. If some of them regretted what became of the Meiji spirit in the flames of Showa militarism, we see how it revived and flowered again in contemporary Japan.

So I would close by repeating Kume Kunitake's definition or criterion of civilization. Travelling through the West, he concluded, as I noted, that it was possible to rank countries in civilization by the degree to which their people shared in the national product.

By those lights the Meiji modernizers left their successors a society much better than the one they inherited. And their followers have improved on that once again.

19

NOTES

1. The Charter Oath (Gokajo no goseimon) text is to be found conveniently in Ryusaku Tsunoda, W. Theodore de Bary, and Donald Keene, eds. Sources of the Japanese Tradition (New York: Columbia University Press, 1958), p. 644.

2. William Elliot Griffis, The Mikado's Empire (New York: Harper & Bros., 1876). ˙

3. Griffis, cited, p. 322.

4. Ibid., pp. 321-322.

5. Ibid,, p. 323.

6. Irokawa Daikichi, Meiji no bunka (Meiji culture) (Tokyo: Iwanami Publishers, 1970), pp. 45ff.

7. Kume Kunitake, Tokumei zenken Bei-O kairan jikki (A true account of the mission to America and Europe) (Tokyo: 1876) v. II, pp. 56-57. See also Jansen, Japan and Its World: Two Centuries of Change (Princeton: Princeton University Press, 1981), pp. 51-68.

8. Quoted in Irokawa, cited, pp. 58-59.

9. Samuel Smiles, Self Help (1859) was translated into Japanese under the title of Saikoku risshi hen (1870) by Nakamura Masanao.

THE JAPAN HELPERS

by John M. Maki

To turn to the outside world deliberately, even eagerly, for the very stuff of the profound internal social change that they sensed confronted their nation was an act of imaginative statesmanship by the leaders of Japan just a century and a decade ago. Who made the decision or how it was made is not clearly known. Indeed, there may have been no deliberate conscious decision.

The question confronting Japan in 1870 can be stated simply: How could the country maintain its political and economic independence and its distinctive social identity in a world dominated by menacing and powerful nation-states which were truly of another world? Logically, there could have been only two answers. First, Japan could attempt to rely only on its own internal resources to develop its powers to the point where it could successfully withstand the challenge from without. Second, Japan could attempt to make its society into a reasonable facsimile of those external societies which, by their very existence, constituted a threat to the nation's independence. The reality of events in the brief twenty years between 1850 and 1870 demonstrated, however, that any logic behind the first answer could not withstand the pressure of practice.

To Japan's intensely pragmatic leaders the circumstances were starkly clear: Japan could not defend itself militarily; Japan was underdeveloped economically; Japan was unequal to the western powers in all respects that counted; and Japan's institutional structure which had served the requirements of the society so well for so many centuries was outmoded. In different terms: a Japan set in the mold of its own history, tradition and culture would fare very poorly indeed in the contemporary world community into which it had been so rudely pulled.

Although there are many unanswered questions relating to the decision to turn outside for the inspiration and the models for a transformed Japanese society, it cannot be doubted that such a decision was made. It was embodied in the critically important five-article Charter Oath of the youthful Emperor Meiji proclaimed in April 1868. The fifth and final article read simply: "Intellect and learning shall be sought for throughout the world in order to strengthen the foundations of imperial rule."[1] That simple sentence raised the curtain on the fascinating spectacle of Japan's turning to the outside world after more than two and a half centuries of isolation from what had become a world in the process of dizzyingly rapid change.

It rapidly became apparent that the fifth article of the Charter Oath was not simply a pious statement of intention, but, in effect, an order. It was the complex series of actions based on that article that proved beyond question that a deliberate decision had been made to turn outward.

A very broad, but not misleading, schematic presentation of Japan's search for "intellect and learning" might contain the following elements: the dispatch abroad of Japaneses students, leaders and others to learn what they could through formal education and on-the-spot observation; the importation of the material objects, the ideas, the techniques and the institutions that were the characteristics of the contemporary world; and the employment of foreign experts to do those things that the Japanese could not yet do for themselves. It is with the last of those processes that this essay is concerned.

What I propose to do is to describe briefly the phenomenon of the Japan helpers or the foreign employees of the Japanese government in the early stages of modernization and then to examine in some detail the experiences of a single Japan helper as an example of how such a one became an interacting element of the complex societal operation that was Japan's modernization.

Foreigners who served the Japanese government have been referred to as "foreigners employed by the government"* or "foreign instructors employed by the government".[+] The former Japanese term is perhaps the more accurate because there were many who where not instructors in the strict sense of the term, although almost all were teachers in that they were performing before Japanese eyes operations with which the Japanese were not yet familiar.[2]

---

* oyatoi gaikokujin
+ oyatoi gaijin kyoshi

According to a table published in 1872 (less than four years after the issuing of the Charter Oath), 214 foreigners were in government employment. The peak was reached at 527 in 1875. Thereafter the number gradually declined until the early 1880's when, even then, more than 200 were still employed. By about 1890 only a small number remained. The foreign employees were a short-lived phenomenon, but their role was considerable.

The 1872 chart alluded to above lists the following positions occupied by foreigners: manager of the mint, language teachers, heads of government departments, illustrators, accountants, tax lawyer, architects, silk spinning instructor, silk mill employees, doctors, military men, teachers, mine foremen, locomotive engineers, carpenters, ship captains, blacksmiths, secretaries, machinery cleaners, lighthouse keepers, shipbuilders, surveyors, and others. The listing provides clear evidence of both the needs of the Japanese at the time and the pervasive activities of the foreign employees.

The distribution of the Japan helpers provides a hint as to the Japanese order of priorities in the early 1870's. The fields with the greatest number of foreign employees were: railroads, 53; lighthouses, 47; shipbuilding and education, each 24; telegraphy, 11; military, 9; and the mint and agricultural development, each 9.

The British were in the overwhelming majority with 119 employees, followed by the French with 50, the Americans with 16 and the Prussians with 8. The British completely dominated three fields, railroads, lighthouses and telegraphy, filling all positions except for a few held by low-paid Asian labor. The French likewise monopolized shipbuilding, filling all 24 positions. Of the Americans six were in education and five made up the Capron mission to Hokkaido, of which more later.

This condensed review of the role of the foreign employees would not be complete without a brief reference to some of the giants among them. Gustave Emile Boissonade of the University of Paris spent 22 years in Japan (1873-1895) and was enormously influential in the introduction of French law into Japan and in the drafting of the Meiji civil and criminal codes. Hermann Roesler, the German legal scholar, first went to Japan in 1878 as a legal adviser to the Foreign Ministry and remained five years to become the most influential foreign adviser in the drafting of the Meiji Constitution of 1889. The American philosophier, Ernest Fenollosa, during the eight years between 1878 and 1886 not only taught western philosophy but played a major role in awakening the Japanese and the rest of the world to the greatness of the Japanese artistic tradition. Lafcadio Hearn as a result of his seven years (1896-1903) of teaching in

Japan became perhaps the greatest popularizer of Japanese culture in the west. There was, of course, William Elliot Griffis whose books revealed much of Japan to many Americans. Finally, there was William Smith Clark, perhaps so far as Japanese are concerned the most widely known of all the employed foreigners.

William Smith Clark, the Japan helper, is the focus of this essay. The concern will be not only with the man himself, but also with the manner in which he became involved in Japan's process of modernization, his peculiar contribution to that process, and the image of Japan he carried away with him after less than a year's stay in the country. It is necessary to examine the man's career briefly because, after all, Clark had already lived a full, rich life for fifty years in Massachusetts, a life which had prepared him, far better than he or anyone else realized, for his Japanese experience.[3]

Born in the remote village of Ashfield, Massachusetts, on July 31, 1826 the son of a country doctor, Clark grew up as a highly active and highly competitive young boy. He entered the first class of Williston Academy in Easthampton, a school founded by the man who was later to become his father-in-law. Following his graduation, he enrolled at nearby Amherst College in the class of 1848. He had already shown a growing interest in science as it was in the 1840's, becoming particularly interested in the collection of flowers and birds. Both because of his youthful interest and the strong influence of two of his professors at Amherst, Clark became a student of science, particularly of geology. Graduated in 1848 after having been elected to Phi Beta Kappa, Clark returned to Williston Academy to teach for two years. He then made the major decision to go to Germany for graduate study. He enrolled in 1850 at Georgia Augusta University in Gottingen and earned a doctorate in 1852 with a dissertation on the chemistry of meteorites, a minor exercise from today's perspective but properly scientific for his time.

He returned to a professorship at Amherst College in analytical and agricultural chemistry and an instructorship in German. Clark soon developed a reputation as an excellent teacher, a leading faculty member and a fund-raiser for the college. But his career as an academic and a rising town leader was interrupted by the outbreak of the Civil War. He became a major in the Twenty-first Regiment of Massachusetts Volunteers and went through heavy fighting, being mentioned in press dispatches for his heroic conduct in battle. He rose to the rank of colonel and was recommended for promotion to brigadier general, but resigned his commission in April, 1863, because his regiment was about to be reorganized out of existence, and returned to Amherst.

Almost immediately after his return Clark became involved in a civic enterprise of considerable moment to his town, the attempt to have Amherst designated as the seat of a new agricultural college in Massachusetts. As a result of the passage in 1862 of the Morrill Act establishing the system of land-grant colleges, the Massachusetts state legislature a year later passed enabling legislation for the creation of an agricultural college. Competition developed among several Massachusetts towns for selection as the site of the new college. Clark, who had developed a steadily growing interest in agriculture between his appointment to the Amherst faculty and his wartime service, devoted his very considerable energies to the twin tasks of winning the planned college for his town and of raising money for its start. Although Amherst won out in 1864, it was three years before the new school was opened with Clark being appointed its president, after he had resigned from Amherst College after fifteen years on its faculty.

Clark was the first active president of the new school, the Massachusetts Agricultural College, although two others had been president during the three-year preparatory period. He envisioned his school as being not simply a training school for farmers-to-be but a true college which would provide both scientific and practical training in agriculture and a broad, general education.

Clark was administrator, teacher and researcher. He built buildings, recruited students and faculty and lobbied hard in the state legislature for the college budget. He demonstrated in his new school as he had at Amherst that he was an excellent teacher, imparting much information with a special eloquence and a degree of showmanship. He conducted and led research that attracted attention both inside Massachusetts and beyond its borders. Perhaps his most scientific work, carried out with the aid of several assistants, was an elaborate study of the circulation of sap in plants. But the experiment that attracted wide attention in the country was one which measured the considerable force exerted by a growing squash.

It would be pleasant to report that Clark's work was rewarded by instant success. That was not the case. Because it was innovative and because it was consuming tax payers' dollars, the new school had to struggle. Clark did, however, succeed in keeping the young college going and even in increasing its size modestly.

By the mid-1870's Clark had become a man of prominence in his town and state and in national educational circles as the president of one of a few land-grant colleges. To those near him he was a man of learning, versed in both theory and its practical application. He was also recognized as being a fine public speaker and an inspiring teacher. He was possessed of an enormous amount of energy, as the outline of his career suggests, and, as his war record showed, of a considerable amount of physical courage. He was also a man whose fertile mind produced workable ideas. Finally, as contemporary accounts and the recollection of associates reveal, he was also impetuous, headstrong, and unable or unwilling to develop smooth personal relationships with others. Fortunately the last traits did not surface in Japan.

Neither Clark nor anyone else had any way of knowing that he was the owner of the knowledge, training, experience and characteristics that were to make him a highly valuable helper of Japan. How, then, did Clark and his tiny school in remote (about four hours by train from Boston) western Massachusetts become gradually drawn into the rapidly unfolding drama of the modernization of Japan, geographically half-way around the world and culturally even more distant?

Clark's first contact with the Japanese came, coincidentally, a few months before the fall of the Tokugawa regime. During his last term at Amherst College in the spring of 1867, Clark had in his chemistry class what he referred to some years later as his "first Japanese pupil." Joseph Hardy Niishima had managed to smuggle himself out of Japan in 1864. He reached the United States and was befriended by the Mr. Hardy whose name he took in part. Later Niishima was admitted to Amherst College from which he duly graduated. Whatever the Amherst ties of the two men may have been, they were strong enough to draw Clark to Kyoto in 1877 to visit Niishima in his struggling school, Doshisha, which had opened shortly before.

In the spring of 1871 there occurred a minor event which was to play a significant role much later on in drawing Clark to Japan, more specifically to Hokkaido. Early in May 1871 Clark received the following letter from General Horace Capron, then U.S. Commissioner of Agriculture:

> I have deemed it proper, in answer to the
> anxious inquiry of His Excellency, Arinori Mori,
> the Japanese Embassador [sic] to the Government,
> for the best educational institution for a Japa-
> nese youth of high rank, to recommend the Massa-
> chusetts Agricultural College. The young gentle-
> man is bright, intelligent, understands English,
> has a fair Japanese education, and is nineteen
> years of age. Mr. Mori expressed some fears that
> you may have no preparatory courses in which to
> prepare him for the regular curriculum. It has
> occurred to me that perhaps in a case so peculiar
> -- one even of National importance, and which
> might also prove of prospective advantage to your

institution -- you might relax something of the
stringency of your regulations for admission, or
at least manage to take charge of the preparatory
instruction of this youth. I shall esteem it a
personal favor if you can accommodate the views
of Mr. Mori.[4]

The "youth of high rank" was immediately accepted (we have
no knowledge of how badly the admissions regulations may have
been bent) and appeared in Amherst shortly afterward. But something must first be said both about him and the other principals
in the letter because they all were eventually involved in
Clark's recruitment and mission.

General Horace Capron (1804-1885) had been a successful
cotton goods manufacturer before falling victim to an economic
depression and then had become a successful dairy farmer. After
a distinguished career in the Civil War at a rather advanced
age he continued his successful dairy business until appointed
the second U.S. Commissioner of Agriculture by President Andrew
Johnson in 1867. He served until 1871 when he resigned to
become the head of a five-man mission to work on the settlement
and development of Hokkaido where he served ably until his return to the United States in 1875, the year before Clark went to
Japan.[5]

The manner of Capron's involvement in the Hokkaido venture
also requires a few words. General Kuroda Kiyotaka, one of the
leaders of Meiji Japan, was appointed in 1870 to the position of
deputy governor of the Kaitakushi (Colonization Commission)
which was in charge of affairs in Hokkaido. He came to the
United States in search of men, methods and materials for the
development of Hokkaido. He met Capron and the two traveled
extensively in this country on inspection tours. Through Mori,
Kuroda arranged an interview with President Grant and requested
advice on the selection of an American adviser for the Kaitakushi. Capron was recommended and accepted the position. Kuroda
was the head of the Kaitakushi when Clark went to Japan and it
was to him that Clark reported.

The youth of high rank was Naito Seitaro who later assumed
the surname, Hori. After several years of study at Massachusetts
Agricultural College he returned to Japan and eventually became
Clark's interpreter in Hokkaido. But of more significance to
the immediate story, he was a close friend of Mori Arinori, who
had earlier taken him into his home in Japan as a kind of
student lodger.

Mori Arinori, referred to as ambassador in the Capron
letter, was actually chargé d'affaires in the Japanese legation
in Washington, but in that capacity was chief of the Japanese

diplomatic mission. It was Mori who was the principal in an incident that drew Clark to the road that led to his mission to Hokkaido.

In the summer of 1872 Mori visited Naito in Amherst. In the course of a tour of the Agricultural College campus under Clark's guidance the two men stood on a slope from which they could see the students in military drill. Struck by the scene Mori immediately turned to Clark, exclaiming, "That is the kind of an institution Japan must have, that is what we need, an institution that shall teach young men to feed themselves and to defend themselves."[6]

Thus it was that an American land-grant college, with its combined emphasis on agriculture and the industrial arts and instruction in military tactics, provided a precise model for Japan. It was especially suited to Hokkaido, which required agricultural development and which was so strategically located in respect to Imperial Russia just to the north and west. It was to be four more years before Clark received his appointment, but Mori's visit and remark did much to assure that the Massachusetts Agricultural College would become the model for what was to be Sapporo Agricultural College and that the president of the American college would become the first head of the Hokkaido institution.

The final actor in the process that was to lead to Clark's appointment was Birdsey Grant Northrop (1817-1898), who had achieved state-wide prominence as an agent for the Massachusetts State Board of Education in the 1860's, and who soon won for himself a national reputation in American educational circles after becoming secretary to the Connecticut State Board of Education. Northrop and Mori had become acquainted during the course of the latter's work to obtain information in America for the Japanese government, which was beginning the important task of establishing a new and modern system of education. Mori was even responsible for an official invitation to Northrop to become chief educational adviser to the Japanese government, but the latter refused the appointment.

Clark and Northrop seem to have known each other most likely though the latter's work with the Massachusetts state board, but it is unknown how closely they may be been associated. At any rate Northrop was involved in the final negotiations in late 1875 which led to Clark's appointment. The extent of that involvement is also unknown. All that survives are Japanese translations of two letters from Clark to Northrop containing Clark's reactions to the proposed appointment. He was willing, even eager, to take the appointment, but emphasized that he could be away from the Massachusetts Agricultural College only one year, not the two that the Japanese government

was requesting. But he boasted that he could accomplish more
in one year than others could in two. The boast turned out not
to be an empty one.[7]

On March 3, 1876 in Washington, Clark signed a formal
contract with Yoshida Kiyonari, Mori's successor as chargé
d'affaires, for the mission to Japan. Clark's contract (there
were both English and Japanese versions) is worth a detailed
look, both for what it tells us about Clark's arrangements and
for what it reflects about the relations between the Japanese
government and its foreign helpers.

The main provisions of the contract were the following:

1)   The period of service was to be from May 20,
     1876 to May 20, 1877.
2)   Clark was to be Assistant Director, President
     and Professor of agriculture, chemistry,
     mathematics and the English language at the
     proposed college.
3)   Clark bound himself to "observe, and, to the
     best of his ability, carry out all the in-
     structions and directions, which may be
     issued from time to time by the Kaitakushi
     officers."
4)   Clark was to work at least six hours every
     day, excepting Sundays and special Japanese
     "resting days."
5)   Clark's compensation was to be "seven thousand
     and two hundred Japanese gold yen" [the equi-
     valent of a like sum of dollars at the current
     rate of exchange] plus a house. Clark, however,
     was to provide the furnishings of the house
     and would also pay the household expenses,
     including the wages of servants.
6)   Clark would not engage in "any trade or
     commerce" directly or indirectly.
7)   The contract could be cancelled on three
     months' notice by either party. If the
     Kaitakushi cancelled, Clark would be paid
     two months' salary following the date of
     cancellation; if Clark resigned, he would be
     paid only for the period actually served.
8)   Clark's travel expenses both ways between
     Amherst and Sapporo would be paid. If the
     contract were to be cancelled while Clark was
     in Sapporo, however, he would receive travel
     expenses only to Tokyo or Yokohama. In addi-
     tion, all his travel expenses, plus those of
     one servant, would be paid by the Kaitakushi
     for official travel in Hokkaido.

9) "The Japanese government reserves the right to
    dismiss immediately the said Clark should he
    neglect to perform his duties, disobey the in-
    stuctions of Kaitakushi authorities, or commit
    any act unsatisfactory to the said Government,
    and in that event, is to pay the compensation,
    to the date only of such dismissal, and the
    return passage shall not be paid by the said
    Government."[8]

The detail into which the contract went provides substantial reason for believing that in the less than ten years that
the new Japanese government had been hiring foreign employees
some difficult problems had arisen which could be dealt with
only by carefully drawn contracts.

Clark left Amherst on May 15, 1876 but his real voyage to
Hokkaido began on May 21 when he and his companions set out from
Philadelphia on the long train trip across the continent and the
still longer trip by ship across the Pacific which began in San
Francisco on June 1 and ended in Yokohama on June 28, almost a
week longer than the average transpacific crossing because of
difficult weather.

Clark was not alone in his mission. Accompanying him, also
on contract to the Japanese government, were two recent Massachusetts Agricultural College graduates, William Wheeler, class
of 1874, and David P. Penhallow, class of 1875. Within a few
weeks after his arrival in Sapporo, Clark received authorization
to appoint a third assistant, William P. Brooks, class of 1876,
who arrived in Sapporo in February, 1877. All three served
Clark exceedingly well during his eight months in Sapporo; all
remained after his departure to work at the Sapporo Agricultural
College; and all three later became presidents of the college.

After a month of conferences, inspection tours, sight-
seeing, and social events Clark and his two young assistants
left Tokyo and arrived in Sapporo on July 31, 1876, Clark's
fiftieth birthday. Clark, of course, had met his superior,
General Kuroda, and conferred with him. More importantly the
two men travelled north together, thus initiating the close
relationship which was such an important instrument in the
success of Clark's mission.

On April 16, 1877, almost exactly eight and a half months
after his arrival, Clark rode away from Sapporo, leaving behind
him a long and almost incredible list of jobs completed. Not
only did he carry out the academic responsibilities called for
in his contract, but within a few weeks after his arrival he
began to function as a principal adviser to the Kaitakushi on
agricultural and other matters with the full confidence and

support of General Kuroda. In addition, in a private and completely unofficial capacity he won all twenty-four members of the first class at Sapporo over to Christianity, their formal conversion coming a few months after Clark's departure.

To evaluate the success of Clark's mission the obvious starting point is to observe the degree to which he attained his principal objective, the establishment of the new agricultural college. There can be no question concerning his success with the school. He and his young assistants examined the young students about whose excellence Clark never tired of boasting; he planned and supervised the construction of buildings; he devised the curriculum and drafted the regulations that governed the conduct of both students and teachers; and he was responsible for the acquisition of both teaching and research supplies.

But his most important activity at the school was teaching. Not only was he (and his assistants) in the classroom four hours a day, but in the evenings he corrected the lesson books of his students. At least several evenings a week he simply sat in his quarters and talked with his students, a valuable form of informal teaching as the students later reported. He also led them on field trips in and around Sapporo. His students often acknowledged in later years the significance to their lives of the impact of Clark both as a teacher and as a model for their conduct.

Beyond the strictly academic sphere of the new college, Clark was responsible for another significant development. Shortly after Sapporo was opened he obtained General Kuroda's approval for the establishment of an experimental farm as an integral part of the new college. It was here that his work as technical adviser to the Kaitakushi was centered. The farm alone would have been a full-time job for most men. It covered 250 acres and its operation included such matters as planning the layout of the farm; building drainage ditches, fences and roads; ordering seeds and farm implements and machinery from the United States; supervising the planting and harvesting; and carrying out various practical experiments.

At the end of less than nine months Clark and his group of three young assistants had the following and more to show for their efforts: a new agricultural college in full operation; a large experimental farm in full swing; a meteorological station; a set of research reports on such products as beer, cattle food, leather, salt beef, forest products, and many others; the instruction of new seeds and breeds of livestock and horses; and, perhaps most important of all, a group of intelligent and eager young students well launched on a four-year program of study and practical field work in agriculture.

All of the students were destined to become leaders in Hokkaido or, more broadly, in Japan itself while a few gained international renown. Their success attested to the soundness of the program and the curriculum that Clark had set up on the model of his own Massachusetts institution and, of course, to breadth and depth of their own intellectual capacities. A considerable and important dimension of their relationship with their <u>sensei</u>, Clark, was the high degree of admiration, respect and, indeed, inspiration that they developed toward and received from him as a man of action, an intellectual, and a spiritual guide.

When Clark said farewell to his students and rode away from Sapporo in April 1877, there occurred a minor incident that guaranteed that he would become one of the most widely known of all the Japan helpers. After a rest and luncheon at Shimamatsu, now a Sapporo suburb, Clark delivered a short farewell speech, which culminated in the brief but ringing admonition: "Boys, be ambitious!" Those three words -- which may or may not have been those actually uttered by Clark -- expressed exactly what Japan had to be if it were to achieve its goal of modernization. One result is that both Clark and his words have become immortalized in Japanese textbooks and so the memory of Clark has remained green to the present day in Japan, although he is a forgotten man both in his state and in his own town.

We have seen what Clark left behind him. But what did he carry away with him? Perhaps of the most obvious importance were the knowledge and impressions of the country that he had gained. But this raises an important question for which there is no answer: What did Clark know about Japan before he set out on his mission?

Unfortunately, we have little evidence on this point. We have seen that he knew a few Japanese students at both Massachusetts Agricultural College and Amherst, but what he may have learned from them we do not know. On the trip across the continent and the ocean he was accompanied by some Japanese, several from the legation in Washington and several who were returning home after stays in this country. Again, we do not know what they may have taught him. He wrote home that one day on the ship he learned the Japanese alphabet. We can only guess that he was referring to his memorization of the <u>iroha</u> syllabary. We do know that he made the decision not to try to learn any Japanese for the practical reason that it would take too much time. Finally, it is a safe assumption that he probably read at least a few of the small number of books on Japan available then to the American reading public.

His letters, his single published account of Japan,[10] and press reports of his talks about the country and its people reveal that Clark acquired a suprisingly large store of accurate information about Japan and the Japanese in a brief period of time. Accurate as much of his information was, it was also curiously impersonal, as if he had only observed Japanese life from the outside and never really experienced any of it.

For example, there were his comments about Japanese food. Shortly after arriving in Sapporo, Clark wrote a report that was extremely critical of Japanese food, clothing and housing as he had already observed them in Hokkaido. His argument was not that they were uncivilized, but that their deficiencies would inhibit the development of agriculture in Hokkaido. He did not mention his own experiences with Japanese food, even though he did refer to "a stinking salt pickle made of radishes." He also was puzzled and even somewhat repelled by what was then the Japanese custom of eating fruit while it was still green and therefore inedible by his American standards. He did develop a passion for <u>mikan</u>, the small, sweet Japanese orange, but that was a product of nature, not of the Japanese cuisine.

His overall impression of Japanese life was extremely favorable. On his return to Amherst he frequently spoke in public about what he had observed, often making comparisons unfavorable to his own society. Unfortunately again, we have no manuscripts of his talks, although some of them were fairly extensively reported on in the press. He published only one article about Japan. <u>The Agriculture of Japan</u> is a 26-page pamphlet published in 1879, the text of a speech given before the Massachusetts Board of Agriculture.

The first part of the talk dealt with Japan and the Japanese in general terms, touching on matters ranging from geography and climate through history to art and handicrafts with some fairly detailed, but still quite general, descriptions. This publication was surprisingly accurate, given Clark's short stay in the country. It has constituted additional evidence of his passion for facts and of his powers of accurate observation, both traits evident since his youth and earlier made manifest in his descriptions of life in Germany in his letters to his family.

Indicative of his strong admiration for Japan is one of his introductory statements in the article that "the progress which her people have made in the last ten years in their political, educational, and industrial affairs, has never before been equalled, either in history or romance." Hyperbole, yes, but still not an erroneous summary of what had been happening.

His comments on the people themselves reveal what can charitably be described as a defective anthropology, but even so contain elements which seem acceptable today.

> The Japanese are a peculiar and remarkable
> race, whose origin and early history are involved
> in obscurity. They are more vivacious, progres-
> sive, and courageous than the Chinese, and have a
> language quite their own. They have a high sense
> of honor, are exceedingly polite and amiable, and
> intensely patriotic. They are apt scholars, in-
> genious artisans, successful farmers, excellent
> sailors, and brave soldiers. They seem to combine
> in their national characteristics, the active merry
> Malay of the South with the intelligence and con-
> servatism of the Chinese, and the substantial phy-
> sique and the Aryan features of the Ainos [sic].
> This union of several unlike races under favor-
> able conditions has resulted in the production
> of a people superior to any of their progenitors.
> As might be expected, there is much diversity
> among them in the form and expression of the
> features, the amount and kind of hair and beard,
> and in complexion which varies from white to a
> very dark yellowish-brown.

Clark's description of Japanese agriculture reveals very clearly why he was attracted to it from the beginning, and not so incidentally why he became so assiduous in his attempts to assist in its development.

> In practical agriculture the Japanese are
> remarkably skillful, and have numerous methods
> and customs which might well be imitated by us.
> There cannot be found in any other country exten-
> sive fields which produce more human food to the
> acre, or which are more free from weeds, or which
> maintain their fertility from generation to gene-
> ration more perfectly, or which more completely
> charm the eye of the intelligent traveller. The
> most important characteristics which distinguish
> Japanese farming are the following: first, irri-
> gation, second, fertilization by liquid manures
> repeatedly applied to the growing crop; third,
> cleanliness of culture; fourth, thoroughness of
> tillage; fifth, constant cropping of lands without
> deterioration; sixth, extreme simplicity and
> economy of method; seventh, the extraordinary
> scarcity of domestic animals and teams with agri-
> cultural machinery.

That perceptive analysis would have been creditable had his mission been solely to investigate the nature of Japanese agriculture. In an earlier talk before the Hampshire Agricultural Society Clark revealed a familiarity with at least some of the working details of Japanese farming to supplement the broader picture.

> The Japanese people are contented, economical
> and industrious. Science follows art, never pre-
> cedes it, and the Japanese have had the art to
> become good farmers without a very scientific know-
> ledge of farming. It would make an American ashamed
> to behold the beauty and order of these farms...The
> work on the farm is done entirely by hand. Cheap
> labor takes the place of domestic animals...Now the
> Japanese is a successful farmer, and the question
> is, how does he succeed without stock to make manure
> with which to fertilize the soil. But the Japanese
> knows how. He irrigates the land by a very costly
> system of canals, he keeps the soil fit for culti-
> vation, then he uses other fertilizers, like lime,
> plaster, liquid manure and fish...Another reason
> why the Japanese keeps the soil in such splendid
> state of cultivation is the fact that he never
> wastes any thing that can be utilized for the
> fertilization of the soil.[11]

But Clark's interests went beyond the soil. He somehow had found time in Hokkaido to acquire information about the Ainu who then were esteemed as being excellent, hardworking guides for the exploration and inspections carried out by the foreign employees of the Kaitakushi. A few months after his return Clark delivered a lecture on the Ainu, supplemented by a display of artifacts that he had acquired, a presentation which was filled with details of their daily life and culture, their accuracy attesting anew to Clark's powers of accurate observation.

Clark also spoke on his missionary work and on Japanese schools. Apparently, he was much in demand as a speaker on Japan, but he seems to have refused many requests for speeches, probably because he had returned to his position as president of Massachusetts Agricultural College and was soon confronted with difficulties far greater than those which had beset the young school in earlier years. It is to be regretted that he never wrote seriously about the Japan he observed and what he accomplished there.

Clark's mission to Hokkaido as a Japan helper was the climax of his career. After his return the financial difficulties of the agricultural college continued to grow and relations between him and his board of trustees deteriorated steadily, culminating in his resignation early in 1879. He immediately became president of a floating college, an interesting educational experiment involving a two-year circumnavigation of the globe under the instruction and supervision of a carefully selected faculty. Clark worked hard on an unsuccessful drive to recruit students, a task undoubtedly made difficult by the $2,500 tuition fee. The project ended in failure with the unexpected death of its financial backer.

Clark then became involved in a Wall Street mining company, the early 1880's being the time of a mining boom. This venture earned Clark a substantial fortune in the course of a year, but it speedily collapsed in utter failure. Clark then became seriously ill, apparently of a heart ailment. The last four years of his life until his death in 1886 saw him completely out of the public eye; he seems to have ventured forth into the town only occasionally. Thus ended the career of the man who is still perhaps the most widely known among the Japanese of all the Japan helpers.

William Smith Clark was only one of many hundreds of foreign employees of the Japanese government in the critically important fifteen years of the initial stage of modernization between 1870 and 1885. How typical he was, both as a personality and as a Japan helper, we cannot know until we have representative sampling of the lives and work of the entire group. But there are some things that separately and collectively clearly set him apart from his fellows: the location of his activities in Japan's remote frontier area, not on the central stage of Tokyo; his role in the creation of Japan's -- and Asia's -- first agricultural college; his triple role as educator, technical adviser and informal missionary; the brevity and striking productivity of his service; the bond of genuine affection between him and his small band of students whose admiration, falling just short of veneration, never diminished; and the plenitude of accomplishments achieved by him and his young assistants.

As a single Japan helper, Clark symbolized the work of the entire body of foreign employees of the Japanese government. He launched a new institution, the agricultural college, an innovation in his own land. He was the bearer of new ideas, science and its application as a technical adviser and Christianity as an informal missionary. And he was a teacher, in the narrow sense within the classroom itself; in a broader sense as the introducer of, and the instructor in, the use of new techniques, new machinery and implements, and new agricultural products; and in the broadest sense as a transmitter of new culture which Japan had to adapt to its own needs.

It was the tragedy of Clark's life that in spite of all his strengths and qualifications he failed to achieve the degree of fame at home that seemed to be rightfully his. It was the paradox of Clark's career that what he did in eight months at the age of fifty won him enduring fame in a strange and vastly different society half way around the world. A Yankee almost inadvertently won in Hokkaido what he failed to achieve in his native New England.

What Clark did he had to do without the benefit of a specific intergovernmental agreement or of the insights that a later social science might provide in the difficult area of intercultural relations or of the massive infusion of cash into the process of society development. Even so, Clark and his small band achieved much. Everything was much simpler in those distant days. But at the heart of their success lay the fact that the help they were so generously offering was being welcomed with enthusiasm and avidity. The Japan helpers were successful because Japan was eager to be helped and because the Japanese were able successfully to absorb what was being offered.

NOTES

1. For a complete text of the Charter Oath (Gokajo no goseimon) see the essay by Marius Jansen, above, and his n.1.

2. This section on the foreign employee is based on the following Japanese sources: "Oyatoi gaijin kyoshi" (Foreign instructors employed by the government), Nihon kindaishi jiten (Dictionary of modern Japanese history) (Tokyo: 1958), p. 65; "Oyatoi gaikokujin" (Foreigners employed by the government), Nihon rekishi daijiten (Encyclopedia of Japanese history) (Tokyo: 1956-60), v. 2, p. 440; and "Oyatoi gaikokujin ichiran" (Glance at foreign employees), Meiji bunka zenshu (Collected works on Meiji culture) (Tokyo: 1928), v. 16, pp. 347-362. The only study in English on the phenomenon of the Japan helpers, as far as is known, is H. J. Jones, Live Machines: Hired Foreigners and Meiji Japan (Vancouver: University of British Columbia Press, 1980.)

3. The material on William S. Clark is drawn from my unpublished manuscript in English, William Smith Clark: A Yankee in Hokkaido, which has been translated into Japanese by Professor Takaku Shinichi of Hokkaido University and published under the title, Kuraaku: sono eiko to zasetsu (On Clark: his glory and collapse) (Sapporo: 1978).

4. As reprinted in the Amherst Record, May 17, 1871.

5. For additional comment on General Capron, see the essay by Donald Roden, below, and his n.2.

6. For an account of the Mori visit, see the Springfield Republican, July 18, 1872.

7. The Japanese translations of the Clark letters are to be found in the Hokkaido University archives.

8. The English and Japanese versions of the contract are to be found in the University of Massachusetts (Amherst) archives.

9. Letter to his wife written on the steamer, "Great Republic," June 5, 1876. Clark's letters from Japan to his wife exist only in typescript done many years later, but both style and content leave no doubt as to their authenticity.

10. The Agriculture of Japan (Boston: 1879), p. 26. The quotation (following in the text) regarding the Japanese as a race appears on pp. 5-6 and that regarding practical agriculture, on pp. 18-19.

11. As quoted from a public lecture and reported in the _Amherst Record_, September 19, 1877.

UNDERSTANDING OF A DIFFERENT CULTURE:
The Case of Benjamin Smith Lyman

by Fumiko Fujita

John Maki's penetrating and thoughtful presentation of
William Smith Clark's experiences in Japan has greatly enlight-
ened us on the important tasks performed by foreign employees in
the modernization of Japan. Among foreigners employed by the
Japanese government in the early Meiji period, Clark was unique
in that he had an electrifying influence upon his students and
had lasting fame in Japan. Compared with other foreign employees, he was also remarkable in having smooth relationships with
Japanese officials. William Wheeler, who accompanied Clark to
Sapporo Agricultural College and became president after Clark's
departure, certainly found working with Japanese demoralizing
and frustrating because they lacked in the "nobility of mind
and character...which is essential to elevating influence."[1]
He thought that Clark had stayed in Japan too briefly to face
this reality.

Here the discussion shifts to the experiences of another
American from Massachusetts, Benjamin Smith Lyman, who repre-
sents a figure in sharp contrast to that of Clark in his relationships with Japanese officials. Thereby, the hope is to
throw some light upon the issue of dealing with and understanding of a different culture.

Benjamin Smith Lyman was a typical New Englander in his
upbringing. He was born on December 11, 1835, the son of a
probate judge in Northampton, Massachusetts. Following his
graduation from Philips-Exeter Academy, Lyman entered Harvard.
Having been graduated from Harvard in 1855, he considered various lines of work, but ultimately chose geology as his life's
work, into which he had been initiated by J. Peter Lesley, his
uncle and an eminent geologist. In 1859-62 he studied in Europe,
first at the École des Mines in Paris and then at the Royal
Academy of Mines in Freiberg. After his return, he took part in

40

various geological and topographical surveys in the United States and in 1870 he was employed by the British Indian Government on a one-year contract to survey petroleum fields in the Punjab, India.

Therefore, no one can deny that Lyman possessed a highly creditable record in his experiences as well as his academic background in December 1872. At that time he entered into a three-year contract with Kaitakushi, a minor department which was in charge of the development of Hokkaido and which was to hire William Clark four and a half years later. In fact, when Joseph Henry, secretary of the Smithsonian Institution, asked Lesley to name a geologist to be sent to Japan, he stressed the point that the man should be "well-skilled in the practical operations of his profession, as well as fully informed in its theoretical principles, of strict integrity, good judgment, industrious habits, gentlemanly deportment."[2] Lesley immediately recommended his nephew, writing that "I know but one person who will meet your numerous requirements."[3]

When Lyman received the offer in June 1871, immediately after his return from India, he declined it "on the ground that the compensation offered [three or four thousand dollars a year with all expenses paid] is decidedly insufficient."[4] He did not agree with Joseph Henry, who thought that "the position should not be viewed merely in regard to its remuneration in the way of money, but also with reference to its importance as a means of extending the blessing of high civilization and more Christianity to a very interesting portion of the human family."[5] Lyman accepted the offer one year later when the salary was raised to seven thousand dollars. Thus his main motive in going to Japan was apparently the remunerative salary. But more deeply was he concerned with his future reputation than money itself; he considered that the work in Japan would be a good chance to establish the geological method devised by Lesley and himself in Japan and to enable him to earn a reputation. In fact, even his concern with the salary seems to have come partly from his recognition that success was often measured by financial success in the United States. When Lyman learned of his father's death, he wrote to his sister that "the beauty of his [father's] character have [sic] not been altogether appreciated by some even of his friends who would have perceived and esteemed them [sic] better if united...to more successful money-getting propensities."[6]

Lyman's first impressions of Japan were favorable. He arrived in Tokyo in January 1873 and was "very well pleased not only with the cordial reception given me, but with the general prospects." Kuroda Kiyotaka, then the deputy director and later the director of the Kaitakushi, was "a very intelligent-looking man" and "especially kind in his manner toward me."[7] When he started to give lessons in surveying, mapping, mathematics, and mineralogy to a dozen of his young Japanese assistants, he found them "so bright, so anxious to learn, so quick at understanding outlandish things, so good-humored, so polite," and teaching them "so agreeable."[8] In the meantime, he began to study Japanese and less than two months after his arrival, he wrote to his father that "I can already make myself tolerably understood...I have got so far as to be able to read children's fairy tales."[9] Although today it is rather hard for those who painfully know the difficulty of mastering Japanese to swallow all of this, his eagerness to learn a foreign language is beyond question.

Lyman worked energetically to fulfill his assignment. During the winter Lyman and his assistants in Tokyo were engaged in drawing maps and writing reports. In April 1873, when the severe winter in Hokkaido was over, Lyman and his assistants left Tokyo for extensive surveys of mineral resources there. They had spent a rough time in the backwoods until winter completely subsided. His assistants were unanimous in their recollections that Lyman was energetic and industrious; he worked as if he did not know what fatigue meant.

While Lyman continued to enjoy friendly relations with his assistants, his relationship with the Kaitakushi officials started to deteriorate one year after his arrival. His distrust for the department was clearly expressed in his letter addressed to an unnamed high official, dated April 16, 1874, in which he demanded the dismissal of a few officials including Kuroda Kiyotaka. While William S. Clark had kept his high respect for Kuroda, considering him as a possible prime minister in the future (Kuroda eventually became premier), Lyman had lost his early regard for Kuroda and became extremely critical of him as being responsible for the wasteful and inefficient operation of the department. Lyman accused Kuroda in a letter to the effect that "he had either connived at robbery of the government or that he has through intellectual capacity been unable to prevent it"; in other words, Kuroda was "either a knave or a fool." Lyman was also indignant over a regulation which required students of the Kaitakushi school to serve the department for many years after their graduation in return for their free education and room and board. Most of his assistants were students of this school and took lessons from Lyman and assisted him in surveys as a part of their school work. Lyman considered the regulation both a "disgrace" and a clear indication that "the right of individuals are not sufficiently respected here."[10] Furthermore, Lyman had been upset because his marriage proposal to a student of the Kaitakushi girls' school was, in his view, interfered with by the school officials. A Kaitakushi document shows, however, that school officials were pleased with Lyman's proposal, taking it as an honor to the school.[11] The seventeen-year-old girl may not have appreciated the proposal from a thirty-eight-year old bachelor, or Kuroda might have in fact meddled in the matter for the sake of a friend, Mori Arinori, who was to marry the girl later. In any case, Lyman demanded the dismissal of two school officials in addition to Kuroda.

Although Lyman's assistants succeeded in persuading him not to deliver the letter, he nevertheless sent two letters to Kuroda, one asking for the revision of the school regulation and the other demanding the dismissal of a junior officer of the girls' school. Lyman's insistent demands and Kuroda's adamant refusal made their relationship sour. Lyman felt that "it is hardly possible...after what has passed between Mr. Kuroda and myself of late, that we could ever have towards each other such cordiality it is desirable between the head of the department and one of its servants; it is not unlikely that he may think it best to release me from my engagements here. If so, I should be on my part more than willing...."[12] Lyman was to work for the Kaitakushi until his contract expired in December 1875. During this period, however, conflicts arose one after another between him and Japanese officials mainly over the control of his assistants and over other minor issues. Each time he demanded his release from the department until he called himself "a Great Resigner."

One of the conflicts occurred in the summer of 1874, when Lyman and his assistants were engaged in surveys of Hokkaido. He ordered a Kaitakushi officer, who had accompanied him as an interpreter, to go with another survey team headed by Lyman's assistant, Henry S. Munroe, because Lyman felt that Munroe would have more need of two interpreters than Lyman would have of one. The interpreter insisted that he ought to consult the Kaitakushi authorities. A ranking official of the Kaitakushi explained to Lyman that the interpreter was accompanying him "in order not only for your convenience but also to accurate [sic] your explanation for our government" and hoped that "you will comprehend our object of ordering him to follow you."[13] This argument did not at all satisfy Lyman, who, regarding the interpreter as one of his assistants, insisted that "there is no court in the civilized world that would not justify me in saying that...in my work I was to have undisputed control of my assistants." Pointing out that he was "serving the Kaitakushi at a great risk to my reputation," he demanded his release.[14] While the dispute continued, Kuroda asked General Horace Capron, the chief of foreigners employed by the Kaitakushi: "I...beg you will use all your influence to persuade him so as to appease his passion." Kuroda wrote that Lyman's order might be a "profitable" one, but that since the order was contrary to the previous one given by Kuroda, "he [Lyman] ought to [have] consult[ed] it with the Department, instead of judging it by himself."[15] Lyman refused to calm down and the Kaitakushi finally conceded him undisputed control of his assistants.

This was far from being the end of conflicts between Lyman and the Kaitakushi. Lyman's growing resentment turned into hostility toward Japanese officials. Considering their attitudes toward him as "a studied repetition of insults," Lyman had "a complete distrust of the Kaitakushi" and "a thorough disgust with its management."[16] The Kaitakushi in turn came to regard Lyman as a burden. Kuroda wrote to Capron: "Mr. Lyman's complaint against this Department was so frequent till now, and he is so disposed as to fight even on so small difference in the business way...it often leads to debar the operation of our work."[17]

When his contract with the Kaitakushi expired, Lyman was employed by the Public Works Department and engaged in geological surveys on the main island of Japan. He thus was to stay in the country until 1881. The experience with the new department resulted in another bitter disillusionment for Lyman because he was overshadowed by a German geologist, whom the department hired as professor of the Imperial University of Tokyo. Lyman gave a warning to a friend in India, one who had expressed an interest in seeking employment in Japan: "Serving them [the Japanese] is like being subjected to a lot of girls -- ignorant, arbitrary, fickle, vain, wilful, faithless."[18]

Certainly the management of the Kaitakushi was not free from inefficiency and mismanagement and thus justified some of Lyman's complaints. Moreover, the Japanese did not make enough effort to explain their ideas fully, partly because they thought their culture was beyond the comprehension of westerners, and partly because Japanese culture has always regarded reticence, not verbosity, as a virtue.

In Lyman's case, however, his fastidious personality seems to have aggravated his relations with the Kaitakushi. He could not ignore what he considered wrong, nor make a compromise. To him, a compromise with the wrong, even in a trifling matter, would have meant degrading him and hurting his reputation. For example, when his contract with the Kaitakushi drew to a close, Kuroda thanked him and sent him gifts, but Lyman firmly declined to accept them. Kuroda, who probably was not accustomed to seeing gifts returned, asked Lyman to accept them, but Lyman flatly refused to do so.

Lyman's experiences in Japan were unique, just as anyone else's experiences are, but they still provide some clues as to how one should deal with a different culture. It is often suggested that learning other people's language opens a window to their minds and feelings. Ironically one of Lyman's major confrontations with the Kaitakushi arose when he felt he could manage without an interpreter. At that time Lyman insisted that "with my imperfect knowledge of the language, there has so far been no trouble while travelling in getting along without an interpreter since more than a year ago, as all the Kaitakushi very well knows."[19] All the Kaitakushi officials did not, however, seem to know it very well. The interpreter in question, for example, said that Lyman's insistence on using Japanese alone inevitably led to misunderstanding.[20] Lyman's case thus suggests that, for all its merits, learning language is not a panacea for understanding other peoples.

In gaining a deep understanding of a different culture, one's attitude is of much more importance than the mere knowledge of the language. Although Lyman obviously tried to understand the Japanese and their culture, he was essentially not different from other westerners who believed in the superiority as well as the universality of their own cultures and values. For example, in his article, "The Japanese Character," Lyman argued that the Japanese "are remarkably quick in perception," and thus "skillful in imitation," but they are "unreflective and not deep in reasoning and originality." Therefore, Lyman predicted that "we may confidently expect that a profound discovery will rarely at any future time be made by the present race of Japanese." In fact, Lyman pointed out, they "have adopted the civilization of others without any important additions of their own." In the field of art, for example, he wrote that they excel in decorative art but lack the profundity essential to high art.[21] Like many contemporary westerners Lyman had a narrow frame of reference based on Anglo-Saxon superiority and generally took the differences in Japanese culture to be a mark of inferiority or a mere object of curiosity.

True understanding of a different culture is difficult, and the difficulty will remain unless one realizes that one's view of another culture is inevitably prejudiced by one's cultural background and that one culture is neither superior nor inferior to another since each has grown from its own unique soil.

Lyman's case also suggests that one needs to have sympathy for an alien people in order to really understand them. Lyman was kind and generous to his assistants and servants; he seems to have been quite comfortable in being paternalistic toward those who depended upon him and followed his orders obediently. When the Japanese were his superiors or colleagues, however, he found his relationship with them awkward. He could not help reminding them that they were backward in the stages of enlightenment. When he did not agree with the Kaitakushi officials, he bluntly told them that his connection with them would be "ruinious" to his reputation and demanded either his release from the contract of their total concession; he resorted to confrontation rather than consultation. Lyman may have been a typical Anglo-Saxon who was, in his own words, "pushing, energetic, forceful, selfish."[22] Too much preoccupied with his own world, he could not consider other people's points of view, to say nothing of their feelings.

Contacts with a different culture, however, bring not only friction but also rewards. The experience of living or working in an alien culture makes one's life rich in various ways. One will widen one's perspective, become more knowledgeable, have more topics to talk about, and gain memories to look back upon. For William Clark in his last unhappy days, the memory of his fruitful experiences in Hokkaido must have been a great source of comfort. Lyman in his last declining days was somewhat cheered up by his continued friendship with his former Japanese assistants, who sent him letters and food as well as money. His adoption of various Japanese foods added variety to his vegetarian dishes and helped him to write a vegetarian recipe book at the age of eighty-one.

Americans, by far the largest segment of foreigners employed by the Kaitakushi, contributed not only to the development of Hokkaido, but also to the long-range friendly relations between the United States and Japan. It is sometimes pointed out that Japanese-American relations have swung from love to hate and from hate to love in the last one hundred years. This may have been so on a diplomatic level, but as far as the Japanese are concerned, under the surface there have been stable, warm feelings toward Americans. One such evidence was a Japanese book on Hokkaido published in 1942.[23] Portions of the book contained much praise for Americans and were even eulogistic in tone. Such a book published during World War II might be regarded as a slender candle in the face of an approaching storm, but still it was warm and bright. The efforts of individuals as private cittizens may not leave a glorious record in history but certainly they are not made in vain.

NOTES

1. Letter, William Wheeler to Irene, February 11, 1878, University of Massachusetts (Amherst) archives.

2. Letter, Joseph Henry to J. Peter Lesley, May 8, 1871, American Philosophical Society, Philadelphia, Pennsylvania.

3. Letter, J. Peter Lesley, to Joseph Henry, May 6, 1871, Library of Congress, Washington, D.C.

4. Letter, Benjamin Smith Lyman [hereafter, BSL] to Joseph Henry, June 9, 1871, Library of Congress.

5. Letter, Joseph Henry to J. Peter Lesley, May 8, 1871, American Philosophical Society.

6. Letter, BSL to Mary Lyman, January 3, 1876, Forbes Library, Northampton, Massachusetts.

7. Letter, BSL to father [Samuel Lyman], January 22, 1873, Forbes Library.

8. Letter, BSL to aunt, June 8, 1873, Forbes Library.

9. Letter, BSL to father, March 9, 1873, Forbes Library.

10. Letter, BSL to Sangi [Councilor of State], April 16, 1874, Forbes Library.

11. School of Kuroda Kiyotaka, April 7, 1874, Hokkaido-cho (Hokkaido Prefectural Office), Sapporo, Hokkaido.

12. Letter, BSL to Horace Capron, April 27, 1874, Yale University (New Haven, Conn.) archives.

13. Letter, Matsumoto Juro to BSL, August 12, 1874, American Philosophical Society.

14. Letter, BSL to Horace Capron, August 26, 1874, Yale University.

15. Letter, Kuroda Kiyotaka to Horace Capron, October 31, 1874, Yale University.

16. Letter, BSL to Horace Capron, December 28, 1874, Yale University.

17. Letter, Kuroda Kiyotaka to Horace Capron, May 15, 1875, Yale University.

18. Letter, BSL to Waterhouse, August 15, 1878, Forbes Library.

19. Letter, BSL to Horace Capron, August 26, 1874, Yale University.

20. Letter, Sato Hideaki to Matsumoto Juro, October 15, 1874, Hokkaido-cho.

21. Benjamin Smith Lyman, "The Character of the Japanese: A Study of Human Nature," The Journal of Speculative Philosophy, v. XIX (April, 1885), pp. 134-135, 137,141.

22. Letter, BSL to Mary Lyman, May 29, 1881, Forbes Library.

23. Hokkaido bunkashi ko (Thoughts on the cultural history of Hokkaido) (Sapporo: Nippon Hoso Kyokai, 1942), passim.

COMMENTARY: on the Oyatoi

by Donald Roden

Recent scholarship has placed the contribution to the Meiji government by American and European employees in a new and exciting light. Previously emphasis dwelled upon the technocratic achievements of the foreign employees and their instrumental role in Japan's modernization: how, for example, individual oyatoi assisted in the construction of railroads, the building of ships, or the establishment of technical schools.

To be sure, the foreign employees played a part in all these endeavors and yet, as has been pointed out, their overall contribution to Japan's emergence in the late nineteenth century was, at most, "marginal."[1] In every agency of state, the Meiji government maintained a firm control over its foreign advisers and thus ·prevented them from assuming a prominent role in Japan's rise as an industrial power.

Does the marginal contribution of the oyatoi to Japan's economic and political development render them insignificant to contemporary historians? Not at all. In his essay, "The Japan Helpers," John Maki challenges us to confront the issues of personality and national character when considering the foreign employees. Maki breathes life into the career of perhaps the most famous nineteenth-century American visitor, William S. Clark. Studies of foreign employees that emphasize administrative position or technical contributions have tended to reduce the employed foreigners to faceless bureaucrats or "live machines."[2] As Maki points out, Clark was clearly more than that.

An enormously energetic and headstrong individual, Clark made a lasting impression upon the Japanese by sheer force of personality. In a brief paragraph, Maki does credit Clark with advancing agricultural science in Japan; but he also reminds us that Clark is most widely remembered for a minor incident at the conclusion of his stay, when the American teacher supposedly bade his students farewell with the stirring refrain, "Boys be ambitious!" The author speculates whether or not Clark actually uttered this phrase. Regardless of the answer, what is most revealing is the Japanese perception that he did. The get-up-and-go ideology of early Meiji* demanded that a prominent foreign authority invoke this slogan. If not William Clark, then someone else.

The quasi-mythic aura that surrounds the originator of "Boys be ambitious" has, as Maki thoughtfully points out, secured Clark a more visible place in the history of Japan than in the history of his own country. The same holds true for other American employees of the Meiji state. For example, General Horace Capron, Commissioner of Agriculture in the Grant administration and later chief adviser to the Hokkaido Development Commission, barely warrants a footnote in American agricultural history; but he is the subject of several books and numerous articles in Japan. Of course, one must be very careful about assigning historical significance according to the volume of printed documents. A cursory glance through relevant bibliographies reveals that most of what has been written about Clark and Capron comes from the period after World War II. Indeed scant Japanese references to Capron before the war are less than enthusiastic. Hence a man who was virtually neglected, or even villified in the 1920s and 1930s, is suddenly immortalized with monuments and belated panegyrics in the 1960s.[3] One is left with the distinct impression that shifting ideological views and diplomatic ties have been more important in sealing the fate of both Clark and Capron than their actual accomplishments as historical actors. Over the past century, successive generations of Japanese observers have perceived the most conspicuous oyatoi as symbols: symbols of "civilization and enlightenment"+ in the 1870s; symbols of imperalist encroachment after 1900; and symbols of renewed friendship across the Pacific in the 1960s. Once again, history tells us more about the changing present than the everlasting past.

The historiographic anomaly whereby men like Clark and Capron are accorded more attention in Japan than in their homeland should not lead students of American history to overlook their careers. For one thing, the spiritual enthusiasms of a William Clark conform to the diplomatic idealism of America's open-door policy. Certainly in the late nineteenth century, the exchange of cultural missionaries served the political interests of a nation that had no pretense of becoming a colonial power in the Pacific.

---

* risshin shusse
+ bummei kaika

50

More important, a study of the lives of American and British employees of the Meiji government might provide a fascinating insight into both normative and deviant standards of late-Victorian behavior. Here we must go beyond the illustrious careers of a Clark or Capron and consider the existence of hundreds of American and British wanderers and vagrant sailors who sought fortune and solace in Japan's port cities. Although the Meiji government initially welcomed the oyatoi as exponents of civilization and manliness, many of the nearly four thousand European and American residents in Japan fell far short of the normative ideal. Tempestuous eccentrics, confirmed alcholics, and, quite possibly, lonely homosexuals were well represented within ranks of employed foreigners, as were the seaport riff-raff -- tramps and roving seamen -- who made up the lumpenproletariat of foreign day laborers. Ironically, and quite unwittingly, the Japanese may have provided an atmosphere of social tolerance that was denied overseas. If so, Japan in the late nineteenth century represented a sanctuary for Western misfits and loners.[4] We need a broad social history of American and European residents in Meiji Japan, for such a study may shed considerable light upon subcultures which are yet dimly perceived in Western historiography.

Needless to say, until social historians are able to unveil the behavior and attitudes of a broad cross section of foreign employees, we are obliged to concentrate, as we have in these essays, on those few, highly literate individuals who not only occupied distinguished positions in the Meiji school system or bureaucracy, but who also served as significant transmittors of information about Japan to their countrymen across the Pacific. Not all of the high-ranking oyatoi were equally skilled reporters, of course. General Capron, for one, vitiated his observations with hopeless sighs that "Everything in Japan is a mystery to me."[5] William Clark, as Maki suggests, was far more dispassionate in his descriptions. Yet as an interpreter of Japan, even Clark pales in significance when stood next to William Elliot Griffis. Although Griffis, as a contributor to Japanese education in the 1870s, was undoubtedly more marginal than Clark, his ability to collect and digest information about Japan was unexcelled.

As noted by Marius Jansen, Griffis' classic study, The Mikado's Empire, stood out as the authoritative interpretation of Japan from the time of its initial publication in 1876 until World War I. Perusing the book today, one is struck by the author's ability to contain ethnocentric references to "Almighty Providence" or "Christian education" and to present arguments that seem all the more remarkable considering the political and social uncertainties of the 1870s. Among his most illuminating observations are a "grudging admiration" of the bureaucratic

machinery of the baku-han* system and a striking recognition
that the Meiji Restoration was more than a simple response to
the West. Elaborating on the latter point, Griffis wrote:

> It is the popular impression in the United
> States and in Europe that the immediate cause of
> the fall of the Shogun's Government, the restora-
> tion of the mikado to supreme power, and the abo-
> lition of the dual and feudal systems was the
> presence of foreigners on the soil of Japan. No
> one who lived in Dai Nippon, and made himself
> familiar with the currents of thought among the
> natives, or who has studied the history of the
> country, can share this opinion.

Instead, Dr. Griffis continued,

> I shall attempt to prove that these causes
> [of the Restoration] operated mainly from within,
> not from without; from impulse, not from impact;
> and that they were largely intellectual.[6]

Unlike so many of his American compatriots, who reduced economic
development to technology from abroad, Griffis recognized the
dialectical force of ideas within Japan's history.

Beyond his insights into Tokugawa feudalism and his views
of the Meiji Restoration, Griffis presented himself throughout
The Mikado's Empire as, to borrow a phrase from Ardath Burks,
"cool, detached, perceptive, and equipped with cultural rela-
tivism."[7] In a particularly revealing passage, Griffis wrote:

> The Japanese are simply human, no better no
> worse than mankind outside. The attempts of good
> people with eyes jaundiced by theological dogmat-
> ics to put so heavy a coat of moral tar and fea-
> thers upon the Japanese as to make them sinners
> above all nations; or the attempt of hearty haters
> of all missionary labors to make the Japanese
> guileless innocents must alike fail before the
> hard facts.[8]

The relentless pursuit of the "hard facts" or "the true picture
of Japan" further distinguishes Griffis from fellow American
writers, notably Lafcadio Hearn who, in 1904, described Japan
as a "fairyland -- a world that is not and never could be your
own."[9] Griffis never accepts Hearn's depiction of a Japanese

---

* baku-han, a compound representing bakufu, the military headquarters of the shogun; and han, the various domains.

fairlyland. "Hearn writes from hearsay," [10]Griffis noted in 1907, "while I saw feudal society as it was."[10]

To be sure, the identification of history with a mere quest for the "hard facts" strikes us as a bit naive today; and certainly William Griffis suffered from no excess of modesty. Still, he stood on fairly solid ground in his critiques of Lafcadio Hearn and other propounders of exoticism. (The latter included Isabella Bird, author of Unbeaten Tracks in Japan, 1881; J. L. Thomas, author of Journeys among the Gentle Japs, 1897; and George T. Ladd, author of Rare Days in Japan, 1910). By his own admission in the preface of the second edition of The Mikado's Empire, Griffis lay no claim to being "the Niebuhr for Japan." But he was a historian nonetheless in his demand for evidence, his relentless collection of source materials, his appreciation of the role of ideas in shaping the past, and his ability to put himself at some distance from the ideologies of his own Pennsylvania upbringing and from the people and events he was observing. A crowning tribute to Griffis the historian was rendered by Ardath Burks in a brief biographical sketch:

> Indeed, it was [his] relative detachment
> which was to set William Elliot Griffis so much
> apart, both in his work in Japan and especially
> in his long career after his return. Imbued with
> a sense of mission, Griffis was nonetheless not
> an ordinary missionary; an alien in a strange
> land, he was sympathetic with the Japanese and
> bitterly critized foreigners; dedicated to de-
> tached teaching and to fundamental research...,
> in political issues he took sides and remained
> a controversial figure. Meanwhile, while he
> taught and preached and argued, Griffis oberved
> Japanese life closely, took detailed notes,
> and reported his impressions in long letters
> written weekly to his sister Margaret.[11]

It is indeed our good fortune, as students of Japanese history, that scholars -- both Japanese and American -- have made William Elliot Griffis and his remarkable collection of materials part of a living historical continuum.

NOTES

1. Clark Beck & Ardath W. Burks, As We Saw Them: Westerners Intepret Japan, 1853-1912 (New Brunswick: Rutgers University, 1980), p. 6.

2. The phrase was used in the title of the study by H. J. Jones, Live Machines: Hired Foreigners and Meiji Japan (Vancouver: University of British Columbia Press, 1980).

3. I discuss the mercurial legacy of Capron in my paper, "General Horace Capron and the Development of Hokkaido: An Historiographic Dilemma," which was presented to the Luce Seminar on Japanese-American Relations at Princeton University in April 1981.

4. Jones has also suggested, in passing, that Japan was an island of social tolerence; Live Machines, cited, pp.77,198.

5. Horace Capron, "Memoirs of Horace Capron," ms., Library of the Department of Agriculture, Washington, D.C.,v.II, p.38.

6. William Elliot Griffis, The Mikado's Empire (New York: Harper & Brothers, 6th ed., 1903), p. 291.

7. Lecture, "The Yatoi: William Elliot Griffis and the Employed Foreigners in Meiji Japan," for the Luce Seminar on Japanese-American Relations at Princeton University in April 1979.

8. Griffis, The Mikado's Empire, cited, p. 570.

9. Lafcadio Hearn, Japan: An Interpretation (New York: MacMillan, 1904), p. 19.

10. William Elliot Griffis, The Japanese Nation in Evolution: Steps in the Progress of a Great People (New York: Crowell & Co., 1907), p. 7.

11. Ardath W. Burks, "William Elliot Griffis, Class of 1869," The Journal of the Rutgers University Library, v.XXIX, no.3 (Bicentennial Issue, September 1966), p.97. A useful, short biography, emphasizing the American background of the educator, is Edward R. Beauchamp, An American Teacher in Early Meiji Japan (Honolulu:The University Press of Hawaii,1976). A young teacher, resident of Fukui, has translated Griffis' Fukui journal:Yamashita Eiichi, Gurifuisu to Fukui (Griffis and Fukui) (Fukui: 1980).

[Addendum]

ABOUT THE CONTRIBUTORS

Clark L. Beck is librarian for the William Elliot Griffis
    Collection, Rutgers University Libraries.

Ardath W. Burks, former Director of International Programs
    at Rutgers University, is now Professor emeritus
    of Asian Studies.

Fujita Fumiko is Associate Professor of History, Tsuda
    College, Tokyo.

Marius B. Jansen, former chairman of the department, is
    Professor of East Asian Studies, Princeton Uni-
    versity.

John M. Maki is Professor emeritus of Political Science,
    University of Massachusetts, Amherst.

Donald Roden is Associate Professor of History, Rutgers,
    the State University of New Jersey.